Original title:
Giggles in the Grove

Copyright © 2025 Creative Arts Management OÜ
All rights reserved.

Author: Colin Leclair
ISBN HARDBACK: 978-1-80567-350-7
ISBN PAPERBACK: 978-1-80567-649-2

Laughter Among the Leaves

In the trees where shadows play,
Squirrels dance the day away.
Birds chirp jokes that soar and glide,
While chipmunks chuckle, tails held wide.

Sunlight filters, warm and bright,
Breezes tickle, hearts take flight.
With every rustle, laughter flows,
As nature smiles in joyful throes.

Whispers in the Woodland

With each step upon the trail,
A playful breeze, a secret tale.
Rabbits hop with giggling flair,
As flowers nod with sprightly care.

Through the brush, a voice does tease,
As swaying branches perk with ease.
The forest hums a silly song,
Inviting all to sing along.

Joyful Echoes of Nature

Every rustle, every sound,
Brings a joy that's all around.
Frogs in ponds create a beat,
While hedgehogs dance on tiny feet.

Amidst the leaves and laughter bright,
Fireflies twinkle, pure delight.
As shadows stretch and twilight nears,
The woodland bursts with merry cheers.

Mirth Beneath the Canopy

Underneath the leafy dome,
Creatures find a place called home.
Laughter echoes through the trees,
Playful whispers in the breeze.

Frolicsome friends in sunlit glade,
Giggling softly, games are played.
The canopy, a giggling crowd,
Join the fun, both bright and loud.

Serenade of Silvery Laughter

In the shade of the leafy trees,
Whispers dance upon the breeze.
A squirrel twirls, a raccoon spins,
Frolic where the fun begins.

Mirthful echoes ring so bright,
Chasing shadows, taking flight.
Through the glades, a giggling stream,
Bubbles rise like a cheerful dream.

Delightful Secrets in the Thicket

Beneath the boughs, a playful game,
Silly critters spark a flame.
Foxes prance, the rabbits race,
Every glance brings a smiling face.

A hidden nook, an acorn stash,
Rolling on in a merry crash.
Cheeky chortles, a joyful sound,
Nature's glee is all around.

Bubbling Joy in the Wild

Laughter spills like morning dew,
As butterflies flit, chasing two.
The flowers giggle, colors bright,
Painting smiles in morning light.

Woodpeckers drum, a merry tune,
While shadows play beneath the moon.
A waltz of leaves, a dance divine,
In this space where joy entwines.

Joyful Antics of Woodland Spirits

Twirling sprites with tiny feet,
Skip along to a rhythmic beat.
Mushrooms sway, a hidden show,
With every leap, the laughter flows.

In bursts of cheer, they dash and dive,
Among the ferns, they feel alive.
Each twinkle of light and frolic here,
A whimsical party we hold dear.

Mirth Beneath the Leaves

In the shade where shadows play,
Squirrels dance in bright array,
Tickles found in rustling grass,
Laughter sneaks, and moments pass.

A tree trunk wears a cheeky grin,
While breezes swirl, they spin and spin,
Puddle splashes, a joyful sound,
Each delight in nature found.

The flowers prance in vibrant hues,
As butterflies wear sparkly shoes,
Bees hum tunes, they buzz and sway,
Nature's jesters, bright as day.

With every twirl beneath the boughs,
Young hearts giggle, nature bows,
In this realm, so light and free,
Laughter sings through every tree.

Frolicsome Breezes

Whispers tease the fragrant air,
As sunbeams tickle without a care,
Frogs leap high, with comic grace,
In this cheerful, playful space.

Winding paths where shadows play,
Chirps of joy lead the way,
Breezes hum a merry tune,
While daisies sway and laugh at noon.

Chasing dreams on feathered wings,
Nature's chorus loudly sings,
Underneath the bright blue skies,
Life unfolds with silly sighs.

From the brook a splashing sound,
Makes friends gather all around,
In the heart of summer's glow,
Frolics dance and spirits flow.

Chuckle Among the Branches

A parrot's squawk, a playful chat,
Makes everyone stop and laugh at that,
A rabbit darts with cheeky hops,
While bloom and petal fall like pops.

Branches sway with secrets shared,
As playful breezes toss and dared,
The earth below, fun-filled and bright,
Each creature joins in sheer delight.

Awkward turtles, slow and loud,
Bring giggles to the walking crowd,
With wiggly worms beneath the ground,
Laughter's echoing all around.

In this boughs and branches' cheer,
Funny moments draw us near,
Nature's humor, calm and sly,
With chuckles heard where friends pass by.

Whimsical Whispers of Nature

Among the flowers, a joke is spun,
In every petal, laughter runs,
Bubbly brooks with splashes bright,
Invite us all to join the light.

Curly vines in a playful race,
Paint the garden with a smiley face,
Sunlit paths with shadows cast,
Invite us in to play at last.

The moon above plays peek-a-boo,
With sparkling stars that laugh, too,
Every corner hums with bliss,
In this world of frolic and twist.

Come join the fun where laughter flows,
In a symphony that nature knows,
With every step, a giggle near,
Whimsical whispers fill the sphere.

Merry Movements of the Meadow

Grasshoppers leap with glee,
As flowers dance in spree.
Butterflies twirl through the air,
Nature's laughter everywhere.

Bunnies play a lively tag,
With a hop and a brag.
Chasing shadows, oh so coy,
The meadow bursts with joy.

Sunshine winks a golden ray,
Pushing cares far away.
Every flutter and sway,
Crafts a tale in bright array.

Children frolic, shrieks abound,
Echoes of fun all around.
In every corner, joy takes flight,
In this meadow, pure delight.

Delight Under the Old Oak

Under branches big and wide,
Laughter finds a place to hide.
Squirrels chatter, tails a-twirl,
While acorns drop with a whirl.

Picnic spread and games unfold,
Stories shared, too much to hold.
The breeze whispers, secrets cheer,
With every chuckle, joy draws near.

Shadows dance upon the ground,
As friends gather all around.
A symphony of playful sounds,
Underneath the oak, joy abounds.

Time flies by in playful glee,
Creating memories, wild and free.
In the comfort of its embrace,
Laughter finds its perfect place.

Harmonies of Happiness in the Hollow

In the hollow, laughter sings,
Magic woven on its wings.
A river chuckles, bubbles rise,
Reflecting joy beneath the skies.

Dancing leaves in rhythm sway,
Tap their feet, come what may.
Woodpeckers drum a lively beat,
Nature's concert, oh so sweet.

Frogs jump in a silly race,
Splashing water, brightening space.
Every corner, a twinkling grin,
Celebrating where fun begins.

In this hollow, hearts grow light,
Every giggle a pure delight.
Sharing smiles, a joyful crew,
Life's a song, and it's all true.

Whimsy in the Wilderness

In the woods where wonder hides,
Playful creatures roam the sides.
Twigs chatter, leaves clap loud,
Nature's antics, quite a crowd.

Mice wear hats, a silly sight,
While owls wink with pure delight.
The stream hums a playful tune,
Beneath the sun and playful moon.

Frolicsome winds play peek-a-boo,
Whispers of mischief in all they do.
Bouncing logs and tickling leaves,
Create a bond, oh so sweet heaves.

In this space of quirky cheer,
Laughter rings, and joy draws near.
Among the trees, a light-hearted spree,
Whimsy dances wild and free.

Joyful Echoes Among the Trees

In the shade, laughter stirs,
Squirrels dance with funny furs.
Branches sway with playful glee,
Nature's jest is wild and free.

Whispers tickle leaf and bark,
Every sound a joyful spark.
Sunbeams laugh and chase the breeze,
Echoes bounce among the trees.

Frogs croak jokes on lily pads,
Witty tales from happy lads.
Nearby blooms chuckle and sway,
Bringing joy throughout the day.

Under skies so bright and blue,
Every shadow feels brand new.
Take a step, and you might see,
Laughter's boundless jubilee.

Chortles Beneath the Canopy

Beneath green vaults of light and shade,
The earth performs a lively parade.
Chirping birds play pranks galore,
While every breeze tells tales of yore.

Giggling leaves rustle and flit,
Nature's punchlines, never sit.
Mossy banks embrace the fun,
As sunlight dances, just begun.

Rabbits hop and share a wink,
In this lively place, we think.
The world is a stage wrapped in cheer,
Where happiness whispers close and near.

A breeze rolls in, like a jest,
Tossing hats from the very best.
In this realm of fertile ground,
Chortles rise and spin around.

Playful Murmurs of the Wood

Amidst the trees, with whispers meek,
Tiny critters play hide and seek.
Breezes send giggles through the glade,
In every nook, laughter's displayed.

The shadows weave a silly dance,
As sunlit ripples ask for a chance.
Mischief twinkles in every sound,
In this playful realm, joy is found.

Woodpeckers drum a funny beat,
While sneaky ants march on their feet.
The branches brush with friendly sighs,
As silly antics fill the skies.

Every creature joins the cheer,
Here, happiness draws ever near.
With every step, the woods can say,
Joyful echoes brighten the way.

Cheerful Shadows Dance

In the glen where shadows play,
Laughter chases clouds away.
Footsteps patter, light and spry,
While giggles float and gladly fly.

Frolicking fawns and dainty thrush,
Share the joy in merry hush.
Twisting vines, with playful glee,
Whisper secrets of the tree.

The sun dips low, creating fun,
As fireflies spark like bits of sun.
With every twirl and bounding leap,
The heart of woods forever keeps.

Laughing leaves in evening's glow,
Twirling shadows, all aglow.
In this dance, so bright and vast,
Cheerful moments forever last.

Sprightly Sagas of the Shrubbery

In the thick of green, they dance and spin,
A squirrel in a hat, with a cheeky grin.
The rabbits play chase, in comedic delight,
While the wise old owl chuckles from height.

Frogs wear their crowns made of lily pads,
Jumping in puddles, oh, the happy lads!
With each joyful leap, a splash and a squeal,
Nature's own laughter — a merry ordeal.

Beneath the Arboreal Arc

Under the branches where shadows play,
The critters all gather to frolic all day.
A hedgehog spills tea, as a fox takes a seat,
While the raccoons battle with strawberries sweet.

High up a branch, a parrot's loud squawk,
Makes everyone pause, they begin to gawk.
The laughter cascades like the leaves in the air,
Joyful and vibrant, it finds everywhere.

Ethereal Laughs in the Wilderness

In the twilight mist, the fireflies glow,
As a catty raccoon steals carrots from woe.
The shadows twist stories in mockery, light,
Painting the night with a whimsical sight.

Beneath the soft whisper of the nighttime breeze,
The crickets compose their tune of unease.
But the moon beams giggle, a cheeky old knight,
Bringing out snickers, both silly and bright.

Larkish Laughter Between the Trunks

Where the tall trees sway, the mischief unfolds,
A butterfly flutters, with tales to be told.
The chipmunks all gather to share their tales,
As the breeze whispers secrets through thickets and trails.

Twisting and tumbling, the leaves join the fun,
With each rustling story, golden warmth from the sun.
Nature's own jesters, in bright hues they prance,
Bringing forth laughter in a cheerful dance.

Elfin Echoes of Mirth

In the woods where shadows play,
Tiny feet bounce night and day.
Whispers dance on leaf and breeze,
Laughter hides among the trees.

Silly hats and mismatched socks,
Twinkling eyes behind the blocks.
Around the bend, a prankster waits,
To leap and tease, it celebrates.

A squirrel grins, with nuts piled high,
While birds chirp a playful cry.
Bouncing through the emerald glade,
Every moment, magic made.

In the twilight, jokes take flight,
As shadows twist into the night.
Elves and sprites of every hue,
Giggling softly, just for you.

Joyful Secrets in the Shade

Under leaves, where sunlight streams,
Lies a world of silly dreams.
Whispers, giggles, secrets sweet,
In the shade, where friends do meet.

A raccoon juggles acorns round,
While butterflies flit and abound.
Tickling tales of grand surprise,
Beneath the blue and cloudless skies.

Laughter spills like bubbling brook,
As every branch holds a funny nook.
Chasing shadows, playing hide,
In this world, pure joy won't hide.

As dusk draws close, the fun won't cease,
The laughter lingers, hearts at peace.
In the darkness, warmth will grow,
With joyful secrets still aglow.

Breezy Tittering Under the Sky

Overhead, the clouds are bright,
Filling hearts with pure delight.
Breezy whispers tickle ears,
As laughter plays like jumping deers.

In the meadow, chums unite,
Sharing stories, pure and light.
A frog hops, thinking it's clever,
While daisies sway, forever and ever.

Bubbles rise from sodden ground,
In each pop, a giddy sound.
With every laugh, the world spins round,
Happy echoes all around.

As evening falls, the stars will gleam,
Again they'll share this joyful dream.
Under the sky, where laughter soars,
The merriment forever pours.

Radiant Roars of Delight

With the sun's bright, glowing rays,
Echoes of joy fill the days.
From branches high, the giggles soar,
With every leap, we all want more.

Bouncing balls and ticking clocks,
Silly pranks with funny socks.
A bear with a hat tries to sing,
And dances around with a bouncing spring.

The breeze carries a teasing sound,
Where smiles bloom and fun is found.
Tickled toes and playful pokes,
Spreading laughter, what a hoax!

As night draws near, and shadows blend,
Every whisper brings a friend.
In the twilight's warm embrace,
Radiant roars spin joy in space.

Laughter and Leaves Intertwined

Beneath the boughs, we skip and play,
A jolly dance, the light at bay.
Branches sway to a cheerful tune,
Nature's stage, beneath the moon.

With every step, the crunch of cheer,
Bright laughter floats, so warm and near.
Leaves rustle soft, a playful sound,
In this merry place, joy is found.

We chase the breeze, with spirits light,
Each tickled branch ignites delight.
Silly hats upon our heads,
As laughter sparkles, mischief spreads.

In twirling leaves, our giggles bloom,
A tapestry of joy and room.
With every twist, the sun shines bright,
In the grove of mirth, we take flight.

Ebullient Explorations

Off we go to wild terrains,
Laughter bubbles like dancing rains.
Curious critters peek and stare,
In our sunny, silly affair.

Through the thickets, we dash with glee,
Imagination sets us free.
Wandering where the wild things thrive,
In this wonderland, we come alive.

Stumbling upon a gnome's hat lost,
We wear it proud, despite the cost.
Sneaky squirrels join in our play,
Creating mischief throughout the day.

With pockets full of secret finds,
And giggles bubbling, our hearts unwind.
Each step we take, a quest unfurls,
In our joyful world, adventure swirls.

Chasing Shadows and Giggles

Shadows dance as the sun dips low,
Chasing dreams as they ebb and flow.
With twinkling eyes, we weave and run,
In twilight's warmth, we find our fun.

Each flicker brings a giggling chase,
Around the trees, we sprint with grace.
Mischievous whispers in the night,
As shadows play, our hearts take flight.

Catching laughs like fireflies bright,
In the dusky air of soft delight.
The moon peeks down, a playful guide,
In the game of joy, we take pride.

Beneath the stars, our spirits soar,
With silly games, we ask for more.
In a world where shadows giggle, too,
We chase the night, just me and you.

Whispered Joy in the Wind

Through the grove, a secret spread,
Joyful whispers dance overhead.
The wind carries tales of delight,
As we laugh till the fall of night.

Sunny patches where smiles grow,
Tickling the flowers, laughing low.
Nature's chorus, a playful sound,
In this gentle place, warmth abounds.

Skipping stones with a gleeful splash,
Creating ripples in a joyful dash.
With every giggle, the world spins fast,
In the breeze, our happiness cast.

Wrapped in moments that softly bend,
In the arms of laughter, we transcend.
With every sigh, the wind agrees,
That joy is found among the trees.

Gleeful Gatherings in the Greenery

In a glade where laughter sways,
Bubbles burst in sunny rays.
A jig here, a twirl there,
Joy dances in the open air.

Chasing shadows, spinning round,
Happiness is all around.
A tickle here, a playful shout,
In this bliss, there's no doubt.

Silly faces, wild and bright,
Every step brings pure delight.
With echoes strong, as friends we cheer,
In this place, we hold dear.

Jests abound, the sun does shine,
Time to play, it feels divine.
We'll savor each bright little tease,
As nature hums with joyful ease.

Heartfelt Hilarity Under the Sky

Beneath the clouds, our spirits soar,
With everyone, there's always more.
A sprightly leap, a quickened beat,
In this realm, we'll never meet defeat.

Silly hats and painted cheers,
Laughter rings for miles, my dears.
With gentle nudges, we tease away,
In this joy, we choose to play.

Tickled pink, we share our tales,
Rainbow socks and funny gales.
Each little quirk is blissfully grand,
Hand in hand, together we stand.

A snapshot here, a snapshot there,
Creating memories that we all share.
In bright sunshine or soft moon's glow,
Our hearty fun continues to grow.

Laughter's Whisper

Under the trees, where secrets dwell,
Whispers of joy break every shell.
A gentle breeze tickles our cheeks,
In silent mirth, it's laughter we seek.

With every glance, a silent jest,
In this haven, we find our best.
Chasing fireflies, a gleeful race,
In the shadows, we find our place.

Mirth and mischief around each bend,
Every giggle, an unseen friend.
We catch the light, we catch the sound,
In this moment, magic's found.

As stars appear in the velvety dark,
Laughter whispers, leaves a mark.
Together we stand, no need to roam,
In our hearts, we've found a home.

Secret Smiles in the Shadows

In the nook where stories blend,
Hidden smiles, on friends depend.
A funny tale shared with delight,
The shadows dance with playful light.

Knock-knock jokes and silly puns,
Turning frowns to joyful runs.
We sway and sway, a whimsical tune,
Under the watch of the silver moon.

Each whispered word, a gleeful tease,
Beneath the boughs, we giggle with ease.
With every step, our worries cease,
In secret smiles, we find our peace.

So gather near, don't pass it by,
Join the fun and let out a sigh.
In shadows deep where laughter swirls,
Let's share the joy, let's change the world.

Enchanted Chuckles in the Clearing

In the glade where shadows sway,
Laughter dances, bright as day,
Trees wear smiles, leaves take flight,
Whispers tickle, oh what a sight!

Squirrels tease with acorn tricks,
Frogs join in with silly clicks,
Sunbeams sparkle, tickle the air,
Joy erupts, banishes care!

Twisted branches sway and twirl,
Nature's laughter makes us whirl,
Breezes carry the playful tune,
Underneath the laughing moon!

What a place, this merry glen,
Come join in, let's laugh again,
Magic spills from every tree,
In this realm, we're wild and free!

Uplifted Spirits in the Thicket

Through the thicket where mischief roams,
Little creatures build their homes,
Their giggles echo, soft and light,
Creating joy both day and night.

Bunnies bounce with furry flair,
Prancing here and everywhere,
Birds exchange their witty jests,
Nature's best, it sparkles and rests.

Every rustle brings a cheer,
Sunset colors draw us near,
In this thicket, spirits rise,
With merry hearts and shining eyes.

Join this dance, let worries flee,
In this world of glee-filled spree,
Where laughter reigns and hearts are light,
Let's celebrate this pure delight!

Delight in the Dappled Light

In the shade where sunlight glows,
Mirth unfolds, the laughter flows,
Dancing beams and sparkly spots,
Chasing away all dreary thoughts.

Winding paths of joy abound,
With silly stories to be found,
Every leaf a giggling friend,
In this joy, our spirits blend.

Butterflies flutter with a grin,
Tickling flowers, they spin and spin,
Nature's jesters, carefree and spry,
Inviting us to laugh and fly!

Step into this playful scene,
Where every moment's light and keen,
In dappled light, let laughter sing,
In this bliss, we have everything!

Whimsy Winding through the Wildflowers

Beneath the blooms in colors bright,
Laughter blooms, a pure delight,
Petals sway to a giggly beat,
Winding paths of joyful feet.

Dandelions scatter with cheer,
Their fluffy heads hold laughter near,
Busy bees hum their funny tunes,
As the sun dips in soft maroons.

Twisted vines with secrets to share,
Playful whispers fill the air,
Larks take wing with hearts so bold,
Spreading joy, a sight to behold!

So roam the meadow, hold on tight,
To every chuckle, every light,
In this haven, laughter grows,
A wild dance where happiness flows!

Nature's Comedic Chronicles

In a clearing where squirrels play,
Bouncing nuts throughout the day.
A rabbit trips, it tumbles down,
And all the birds just laugh and frown.

A clever crow tells a joke,
As a tree stump starts to poke.
The deer all chuckle, rolling near,
While the frogs croak loud, we cheer!

The ants are marching on a spree,
Dancing in time, oh what a glee!
With every step, they trip and slide,
Creating chaos far and wide.

As shadows stretch into the night,
The moonlight plays a funny sight.
Fireflies flicker with delight,
Nature's humor shines so bright.

Fables of Fun in the Foliage

Once a fox donned a silly hat,
That made him look just like a cat.
With every pounce, he'd lose the thing,
And the laughter flew on feathered wing.

A turtle spun in a wild race,
With its shell there's no such pace.
Yet all the critters gathered round,
To watch the slowest sprinting sound.

In the thicket, a wise old owl,
Recited tales with a chuckling howl.
He mixed up facts in such a way,
We questioned what was night or day.

With each new tale from leaf to vine,
The laughter grows, the spirit shines.
For in this wood, where stories live,
The greatest gift is joy to give.

Merriment in the Moss

The mossy carpet hid the fun,
Where turtles slid and mushrooms spun.
Each critter laughed, they blended well,
In a pocket of joy, all hearts swell.

A chipmunk danced on a fallen log,
To the rhythm of a chirping frog.
With every twirl, a bush did shake,
As laughter echoed, make no mistake.

A windy gust tossed leaves like toys,
While beetles played with joyful noise.
The stream chuckled, a bubbly rhyme,
In this joyous place, we share our time.

Sprinkled sunlight through boughs above,
Embraced by nature, full of love.
In this space, where laughter flows,
Mossy magic, everybody knows.

Blissful Banter by the Brook

By the brook where the water sings,
A family of ducks flaps their wings.
With a splash, one dove for a drink,
And the others paused just to blink.

A playful otter whooshed on by,
Riding currents, oh so spry!
He tumbled back with a frothy grin,
As the fish laughed, letting joy in.

Crickets chirped their silly song,
While a snail sauntered slowly along.
Every twist and turn brought cheer,
As the world around us reappeared.

With the sun setting low and fair,
We share our tales beyond compare.
In this moment, with friends we play,
The brook hums softly, come what may.

Cheery Notes in the Forest

In the shade, the squirrels dart,
Chasing tales, a playful art.
With every jump and twisty spin,
Laughter echoes loud within.

A chatterbox of birds take flight,
Tickling leaves in pure delight.
The bunnies hop in silly pairs,
As nature laughs, without any cares.

Oh, to dance with joy and cheer,
Each rustle brings a giggling ear.
While butterflies spin in the sun's glow,
They twirl and dip, stealing the show.

A tap on wood, a giggle quick,
The forest hums a playful trick.
As dappled light breaks through the green,
It's a happy scene, so bright and keen.

Lively Treetop Tales

The leaves whisper secrets, soft and sweet,
As acorns tumble, a cheerful beat.
The raccoons wear masks with flair and style,
Swirling around, they make us smile.

Up high, the owls hoot with glee,
Telling stories of silliness, just for me.
A parade of frogs, hopping along,
In their own rhythm, a silly song.

Each branch offers a stage so bright,
Where critters play from day to night.
The forest lives with laughter's sound,
As funny tales are spun all around.

A dance of shadows, a jolly spree,
Nature's jesters, wild and free.
In the canopy, the fun takes flight,
With joyful hearts, we share delight.

Sunny Laughter in the Dappled Light

On sunlit paths where wildflowers bloom,
Bumbling bees create quite the room.
Tickled pink by a breeze so light,
They whirl like dancers, pure delight.

The foxes prance with a skip and a hop,
Playing peek-a-boo, they just can't stop.
While daisies blush in shades of glee,
Laughter rings out from every tree.

In dappled light, shadows grow long,
Each rustling leaf hums a happy song.
The world's a stage, the trees the cast,
Moments of joy, forever to last.

A squirrel slips, a gentle fall,
Bouncing back with a breezy call.
As the sun sets and the colors blend,
The laughter lingers, a joyful trend.

Glimmers of Glee Among the Pines

Among the pines, a hidden show,
With giggling echoes, sweet and low.
The chipmunks chatter in cheeky tones,
While shadows dance on the laughing stones.

A riddle played on the swaying breeze,
The forest chuckles, rustles the leaves.
With every step, a story unfolds,
Of mishaps and charms the wild forest holds.

In every nook, joy hides and peeks,
Tickling fawns, igniting squeaks.
Branches sway as the critters play,
Filling the world with laughter's array.

Laughter bubbles through every pine,
As harmony weaves in nature's design.
Amidst the trees, we dance and sing,
In this grove, where joy takes wing.

Lighthearted Larks in the Land

In fields of green, where laughter sings,
Small critters dance with flapping wings.
Chasing clouds on sunny days,
The world spins round in funny ways.

Bouncing balls and playful shouts,
Hide and seek with silly bouts.
With every twist, a chuckle flows,
As joy in every corner grows.

Mirthful tunes by the babbling brook,
Join the frolics, come take a look.
Silly hats and mismatched shoes,
In laughter's realm, we just can't lose.

Underneath the bright blue skies,
All worries fade, and laughter flies.
So come join in this cheerful cheer,
In this merry land, all hearts are here.

Whimsy of the Whispering Woods

Beneath the leaves where antics creep,
The forest hums with secrets deep.
Squirrels prance with nuts in tow,
While trees give whispers, soft and low.

A raccoon dons a flower crown,
And toadstools grow all around.
The mice hold court in fine attire,
As chuckles rise like smoke from fire.

With every breeze, the branches sway,
Tickling magic where creatures play.
Echoes of joy in every glade,
A symphony of chuckles made.

So come and stomp through leaf and twig,
Join the festivities, dance a jig.
In these woods where laughter sways,
Each moment here is a joyous blaze.

Serene Snickers of the Savanna

Across the plains where zebras roam,
A playful breeze feels like home.
The sun dips low, a golden ball,
While cheeky monkeys commence a brawl.

With every leap and cheeky throw,
The laughter sparkles like the glow.
Meerkats pop from sandy dens,
In soft giggles, they meet their friends.

As wildebeests gallivant about,
The air bursts forth with joyful shouts.
A dance of sprites on grass so wide,
In this wild charm, we can't confide.

So let your heart be light and free,
Join the fun where all can see.
In this savanna, tales unwind,
With every laugh, more joy we find.

Rhapsody of the Rustling Foliage

Among the leaves, a story stirs,
Where laughter's whisper softly purrs.
The wind weaves tales through branches vast,
As nature steals the silliness fast.

A chubby rabbit hops with glee,
Chasing shadows, wild and free.
The daisies giggle at the joke,
As swirling petals float and poke.

Each rustle prompts a joyous sound,
A playful jest from the ground.
Silly squirrels play peek-a-boo,
Causing smiles in the morning dew.

With every rustle and lighthearted cheer,
The forest thrives on fun so near.
So roam these woods, take time to play,
In this rhapsody, we'll laugh all day.

Radiant Ribbons of Laughter

In the bright beam of sun, they play,
Puppies chase shadows all day.
Silly hats set afloat on a breeze,
With each step, the world bends at ease.

Bouncing balls and playful sighs,
Children's giggles meet the skies.
Each flower spreading joyful cheer,
Whispers of joy for all to hear.

Chasing after butterflies' whims,
Their laughter dances like flowing hymns.
A playful tug on a grateful shoe,
In this place, dreams always come true.

Tickles abound in nature's hold,
A tapestry of tales unfolds.
Around every corner, a new jest waits,
In the grove of fun, happiness creates.

Chirping Chortles in the Meadow

Little birds tweet, a raucous cheer,
Nature's jesters, always near.
With every hop, a jumpy dance,
A painted world of sheer romance.

Ladybugs in a grand parade,
Winks exchanged in sunlight's shade.
Grasshoppers hopping, tasks undone,
In every corner, laughter spun.

Silly frogs on lily pads bask,
With ribbits that make you ask,
If joy can be wrapped like a bow,
In the heart's meadow where chuckles flow.

Sunbeams twirl on a bright green stage,
Each silly step, life turns a page.
Chortles echo through the fields,
In this laughter, the heart yields.

Tickled Roots of the Earth

Beneath the grass, in cozy nooks,
The roots of cheer hold secret books.
Each whisper of wind, a playful tease,
Among the trees, joy finds its ease.

Squirrels dash with a raucous spin,
Chasing each other, let the fun begin.
Mischievous breezes tickle the leaves,
In the woodland's arms, laughter weaves.

Tiny ants march in straight lines,
With funny hats, they contrive designs.
Crickets chirp a merry song,
In the harmony where all belong.

Earth's laughter ripples, a quirky dance,
Inviting all to join the chance.
With roots entwined in playful jest,
This is where we find our quest.

Laughter at the Edge of Twilight

As day bids farewell, shadows emerge,
A giggle floats on the night's verge.
Fireflies flicker like stars at play,
In the cool air, smiles find their way.

Whispers weave through the darkening glade,
Echoes of chortles serenely parade.
Bats swoop low in a swoosh and glide,
As the world can't help but giggle inside.

A soft breeze carries secrets of fun,
In every rustle, the joy's never done.
With each glance of the Moon's silver grin,
The laughter grows within and spins.

At twilight's door, the spirit runs free,
In the night's embrace, let it be.
Where shadows dance, and hearts collide,
In the laughter shared, we all abide.

Fanciful Frolics of the Fey

In the thicket where shadows play,
Little sprites dance and sway.
With mischief twinkling in their eyes,
They craft new laughs that never die.

A squirrel scurries, just for fun,
Chasing shadows in the sun.
With every leap, and every bound,
A chorus of giggles spins around.

The flowers giggle, tickled by breeze,
As whispers travel through the trees.
In moments caught, the world feels light,
Their antics make the day feel bright.

So if you wander, stop and see,
These playful, laughing company.
For in their realm of joyful play,
Each chuckle greets the dawn of day.

Cheer from the Canopy

Above the ground where branches sway,
The chirping birds begin to play.
They sing of pranks and silly things,
As laughter drips from feathered wings.

A raccoon sneaks with a plastic hat,
He tumbles softly, just like that!
With each mishap, a sound so bright,
Echoes burst into the night.

The sunbeams dance upon the leaves,
Each ray a spark that never grieves.
In every corner, joy resides,
Where happiness in shadows hides.

Listen closely as they cheer,
The forest whispers, "Come draw near!"
For in this lively verdant space,
Laughter shines on every face.

Laughter Like Leaves in the Wind

When the morning sun does peep,
The giggle winds softly sweep.
Leaves flutter down like tiny sprites,
Spreading joy in playful flights.

In the bramble, mischief grows,
Whispers dance, and laughter flows.
With playful nudges, friends collide,
Rolling in happiness, side by side.

A turtle stumbles, a twisty fall,
And all around, the giggles call.
With every moment, they spin and twirl,
A tapestry of joy unfurl.

So join the fun in this merry spree,
Where laughter rules the ancient tree.
For in this haven of joyous sound,
A sibling charm in nature is found.

Happiness Hiding in the Hollow

In a hollow where secrets dwell,
Nature hides its laughing spell.
A rabbit hops with a grin so bright,
Chasing chuckles into the night.

Twinkling fireflies join the dance,
Every flicker a chance, a chance!
To unveil joy beneath the dawn,
Where laughter plays and worries are gone.

A gentle breeze can't help but tease,
Wrapping all in giggly ease.
The mushrooms chuckle, the streams they sing,
As little ones revel in everything.

So venture down the winding way,
Join the mirth where shadows sway.
For happiness, in corners shy,
Will lead you straight to the sky.

Fanciful Frolics in the Forest

In the glade where shadows play,
A squirrel dances all the way.
With acorns flying through the air,
There's laughter drifting everywhere.

Beneath the trees, the raccoons prance,
Chasing fireflies in a trance.
A chorus of chirps breaks the night,
As creatures join in pure delight.

Frogs in puddles jump and splash,
While butterflies in colors flash.
The breeze carries a joyful tune,
As smiles bloom like springtime's moon.

Every leaf holds a secret jest,
A hidden joke, a playful quest.
In each twist, in every turn,
The forest's laughter starts to burn.

Chortles Under the Boughs

Beneath the canopy so wide,
Where critters scamper, slip and slide.
A chorus of giggles fills the air,
As branches sway with playful flair.

The woodpecker knocks a silly beat,
While rabbits hop on tiny feet.
Each rustle brings a chuckle low,
As mushrooms dance in a row.

The sunset paints the sky so bright,
While owls hoot with sheer delight.
A raccoon juggles, quite the show,
In the heart where laughter flows.

With every breeze, a giggle twirls,
Among the ferns, the fun unfurls.
The woodland spirits laugh and sigh,
As colors flash and moments fly.

Bubbles of Bliss Amidst the Trees

In a patch where sunlight bursts,
Little fairies quench their thirst.
With giggles sweet and hearts so light,
They dance away into the night.

A hedgehog rolls down a grassy knoll,
Creating laughter, bright and whole.
The bumblebees join in the fun,
Buzzing tunes 'til day is done.

Mice in hats waltz hand in hand,
While mushrooms bob to a band.
The whispers echo, soft and clear,
As joy and mirth draw ever near.

The stars peek through the leafy dome,
In this playful, happy home.
Their shimmer makes the laughter soar,
As the woods sing forevermore.

The Secret Smiles of the Sylvan

In the woods where shadows glide,
　Mysteries are tucked inside.
The trees chuckle, the bushes grin,
　As they echo where fun begins.

A bunny's hop, a chipmunk's twist,
　In every nook, a joyful gist.
The petals sway with cheeky grace,
　As laughter fills this secret space.

Winking stars peek from above,
　Casting magic, warmth, and love.
Every whisper holds a cheer,
In the sylvan realm, there's no fear.

So join the frolic, let it grow,
　In the forest's vibrant show.
With every step, the joy expands,
　In this land of merry bands.

Serendipity in the Soil

A worm wore a hat, what a sight,
He danced in the dirt, full of delight.
A beetle with stripes sang a tune,
While flowers chuckled, sun and moon.

Caterpillars spun spinning tales,
As ants told stories of grand scale.
The breeze joined in with a gentle hum,
Laughter echoed, oh how it did come!

Mushrooms formed a quirky band,
Tapping their caps, oh so grand.
The soil held secrets light as air,
Every little creature joined the affair.

As dusk fell down, the stars did pop,
An owl swooped by with a funny plop.
Each root and leaf wore a silly grin,
In this merry world, we all fit in.

Sunlit Chuckles Among the Flora

In the garden where daisies sway,
A squirrel juggled nuts all day.
Petals giggled in the warm breeze,
While groundhogs made merry, aiming to tease.

Bumblebees buzzed with rhythm so sweet,
Doing a dance with their tiny feet.
A ladybug laughed, quite a sight to see,
As it twirled with glee, wild and free.

Sunflowers stood tall with grins so wide,
Tickling each other, they'd never hide.
A playful breeze sent shadows in play,
Laughter spilled forth, what a fine day!

Among the green, fun has its way,
Goofy moments brighten the fray.
Nature whispers with a cheeky gleam,
Join in this laughter, live the dream!

Joyous Shadows on the Path

On the winding path where shadows blend,
A rabbit hopped, a true best friend.
With each leap, shadows danced along,
Creating a rhythm, a playful song.

Ducks waddled by with winks and nods,
While bees held court with tiny odds.
The sunbeams giggled, lighting the way,
Casting silly shapes in a brilliant play.

A fox spun tales, weaving a yarn,
While trees clapped hands, their barks like charm.
With every step, the ground would tease,
Inviting all souls with laughter's ease.

Underneath the arch of leaves so grand,
We found treasures that laughter planned.
In shadows of joy, we'll joyfully roam,
Every path leads us closer to home.

Nature's Playful Palette

Colors splashed in a joyful spree,
A parrot squawked, "Come laugh with me!"
Roses giggled as they bloomed wide,
While violets whispered, filled with pride.

Breezes painted the air with cheer,
Each flower swayed, pulling near.
The brook babbled secrets, giggling low,
Echoed by crickets putting on a show.

The sun wore glasses, oh what a sight,
A butterfly danced in pure delight.
Clouds joined in with artful moves,
Nature's hues, a canvas that grooves.

With laughter and joy, the world can sway,
In this palette where wishes play.
Let's splash our hearts across the sky,
Together we'll sing, let our spirits fly!

Breezy Belly Laughs in the Wilderness

In the rustling leaves they play,
Silly critters dance away,
Jumping squirrels chase their tails,
Laughter echoes on the trails.

A raccoon in a funny hat,
Dances with a sleepy cat,
The sunbeams twinkle, shadows prance,
Nature's joyful, wild romance.

Frogs croak out a comic tune,
Crickets join beneath the moon,
Every stone holds a joke untold,
A forest full of laughter bold.

Through the branches, giggles soar,
Each new step reveals much more,
With friends in shades of green, we find,
A wilderness of laughter, beautifully aligned.

Humor of the Hidden Glade

In the clearing, a clownish deer,
Tells corny jokes, makes all cheer,
While butterflies pirouette with glee,
The trees sway with mirth, wild and free.

A bumblebee wears mismatched shoes,
Buzzing out the latest news,
The flowers giggle in blushing hues,
As nature plays, no time to lose.

Mice play tag with windy red kites,
Chasing shadows, scaling heights,
Their laughter peels through the fresh air,
In this glade, humor's everywhere.

A turtle slips on a well-worn log,
Sending ripples with a splashy smog,
The hidden glade, where chuckles reside,
A secret spot where joy won't hide.

Tickles from the Timberline

Up at dusk, the tall pines sway,
With giggles drifting far away,
A squirrel with a wig on tight,
Stirs up chuckles in fading light.

Owls with glasses, wise and round,
Share the funniest tales around,
Each whoo reveals a punchline snappy,
Tickles dance, making all happy.

The stream gurgles a playful rhyme,
Puppies frolic, chasing time,
Every rock holds a secret song,
In the timberline where we belong.

Laughter bubbles like the brook,
In these woods, take a happy look,
Nature's jesters, merrily blend,
With humor that will never end.

Joyful Jests Among the Pines

Among the pines, a party brews,
Where shadows play, and light imbues,
A porcupine with a goofy grin,
Picks the best pranks, let the fun begin.

Chirping birds in a comic row,
Sing in harmony, put on a show,
Their tunes bounce off each fragrant pine,
Crafting laughter that feels divine.

Bunnies hopping, full of cheer,
Springing forth, they sound like deer,
With each bound, a new joke is made,
In this playful, leafy parade.

Even the clouds let out a chuckle,
As they drift past, bright and snuggle,
Among the trees, fun thrives and shines,
In a world of joyful jests so fine.

Silly Ramblings on the Trail

A squirrel wore a tiny hat,
Chasing shadows, what of that?
With every hop and every leap,
A chuckle stirred, from smiles it'd seep.

A rabbit danced with flopping ears,
Tickling toes and hearty cheers.
The route was wild, with whimsy bright,
Each twist and turn pure delight.

We stumbled on a frog in shoes,
Croaking jokes none could refuse.
It sang of flies and morning mist,
Leaving behind a laugh-filled twist.

So off we traipse, our spirits high,
Where laughter's magic fills the sky.
In dance of joy, we spin and twirl,
Among the trees, life's fun unfurl.

Cascades of Smiles

The brook giggled by the stones,
Whispers sweet and playful tones.
A breeze tickled leaves on trees,
Causing mischief with such ease.

A frog in a crown flashed a grin,
Wearing chaos like a win.
With each splash of water, new joy,
Who knew nature could be so coy?

The sun peeked through with a wink,
Made flowers sway, began to think.
Petals danced on the water's crest,
Nature's jest, it did its best.

Laughter bubbles, a river of light,
In a world that feels just right.
With each smile, down it flows,
A cascade of cheer, where fun grows.

Pint-Sized Laughter in Blossoms

In a flower patch, so bright and bold,
Tiny creatures, stories told.
Ants in a line with hats of green,
Marching in sync, a funny scene.

A ladybug played hide-and-seek,
Peeking 'round petals, oh so cheek!
While butterflies giggled, flapped their wings,
In the warm sun, the joy it brings.

A bumblebee buzzed a silly tune,
Making sweet the afternoon.
Every bloom wore a happy face,
In this merry, vibrant place.

Whispers of joy in the warm air,
Laughter wrapped in nature's care.
Together they danced, a joyful squad,
In blossoms' embrace, we all applaud.

Rustling Revelry

Leaves shared secrets on the breeze,
Rustling softly as they tease.
A playful fox tipped its hat,
With a grin that made us laugh at that.

The shadows danced upon the ground,
Whimsical shapes all around.
A bear with a wig lolled in glee,
Exclaiming, "What a sight to see!"

Acorns dropped with little thuds,
Each one bringing silly floods.
A raccoon laughed, in full delight,
As giggles echoed through the night.

In meadows where the wild things play,
Joy floats like it's here to stay.
With each rustle, there's a cheer,
In nature's revelry, we hold dear.

Echoes of Fun in the Ferns

In the shade where laughter springs,
Frogs play tunes with vibrant strings.
Bouncing beetles, quick as light,
Twirl around, a joyful sight.

Squirrels chatter, thoughts so bright,
Stashing nuts, they're quite the sight.
With winks and wiggles, they parade,
Nature's stage, the perfect stage.

Whispers tickle between trees,
Dancing breezes stir the leaves.
While shadows play peek-a-boo,
Every moment feels so new.

A chorus hum of blissful cheer,
With every rustle, draws us near.
Laughter echoes in the glade,
A memory none will trade.

Whirl of Whimsy Among the Roots

Beneath the arches where the wildflowers bloom,
Mice on tiny roller skates zoom.
Tails entwined in a chaotic dance,
Every creature takes a chance.

Blissful breezes pull on hats,
As playful sparrows tease the cats.
The old tree trunk, a jolly throne,
Hosts a party, all alone.

Fiddling crickets serenade the night,
While ghostly fireflies twinkle bright.
Ember logs serve s'mores with glee,
As laughter's the sweetest melody.

Round and round, the circle spins,
With every twist, the fun begins.
And if you trip, just smile and say,
The roots have tangled you in play.

Blissful Chimes of the Woodlands

Checkered shadows paint the ground,
Happy whispers all around.
Leaves drape down like silly hats,
As kittens chase the chipmunk's spats.

In the glen where giggles blend,
Waffles serve as the perfect trend.
Jellybeans tumble from the trees,
A feast awaits in the gentle breeze.

Mirthful echoes, every cheer,
Brings the woodland critters near.
Shimmering lights twinkle and sway,
Creating joy in a breezy ballet.

With each tick of the settling sun,
The woodland's laughter is never done.
In every nook, a smile resides,
A treasure where pure joy abides.

Smiles Showered by the Sun

Sunshine spills like liquid gold,
Tickling toes, the air is bold.
Jolly fawns skip across the way,
While blooms stretch and sway in play.

Rabbits wear their Sunday best,
As they hop with zest and jest.
Clouds drift by, with playful grace,
Carving smiles on each tiny face.

Breezes wrap around the trees,
Whispering secrets with the breeze.
Joyful moments, one by one,
Dance like rays of morning sun.

Pinecone races down the hill,
While laughter rings, a perfect thrill.
With sunshine warm and spirits high,
The world's a playground, oh my, oh my!

Swaying Spirits of Cheer

In the trees, a whisper sings,
A dance of joy, a rhythm springs.
Branches sway, tickling the air,
Laughter blooms everywhere.

Beneath the sun, a playful breeze,
Jumps around with lively ease.
Squirrels peek from their leafy homes,
Chasing shadows where laughter roams.

Bouncing balls of light collide,
Gentle giggles can't be denied.
With each step, the ground shakes bright,
As smiles burst into sheer delight.

In this grove, the spirits play,
Frolicking through the bright array.
A gathering of joy divine,
Where every heart is free and fine.

Mirthful Moments in the Greenery

Underneath the canopy's shade,
Little critters laugh and wade.
Flowers nod their heads in glee,
Welcoming all who come to see.

Chirping birds join in the cheer,
Fluffy tales we long to hear.
Funny faces on the trees,
Winking at us in the breeze.

Frogs croak jokes, a playful tease,
They bounce around with such sweet ease.
The sunbeams dance upon the ground,
A symphony of joy resound.

Moments shared, the laughter grows,
In the greenery, anything goes.
With every step, the spirit glows,
In this place where happiness flows.

Flutter of Feet in the Forest

Pitter-patter on the trail,
A merry tune begins to sail.
Leaves rustle with a giggly sound,
As tiny feet prance all around.

Bouncing bunnies hop and play,
In a world where joy leads the way.
Chasing shadows of the afternoon,
Laughter twirls beneath the moon.

Swaying grasses break into song,
As we frolic, it won't be long.
Twirling in this lively dance,
Where every glance is a merry chance.

The forest floor, a stage so bright,
Welcomes all to join the flight.
With each flutter, the spirits soar,
In this fun, we all want more.

Radiance of the Happy Hour

As the sun dips low at dusk,
Giggles spark; it's a must.
Gathered 'round the vibrant glow,
Stories shared as breezes flow.

Laughter bubbles like a stream,
The air is light; the world a dream.
Jokes unfold like petals rare,
Unleashing joy that fills the air.

With every chuckle, spirits rise,
The night delights with playful skies.
Toasting to the laughter's cheer,
Moments cherished, year by year.

In this hour, the hearts align,
With silly tales, we intertwine.
A radiant night in nature's arms,
Where joy is wrapped in sweet charms.

Sunny Shenanigans Under the Branches

Laughter echoes through the trees,
Squirrels dance with the buzzing bees.
Wobbling branches sway and swirl,
As sunlight bounces, twirls, and whirls.

Ticklish leaves tickle the ground,
With each breeze, smiles abound.
Playful shadows leap and race,
In this cheerful, lively place.

Chasing shadows, we forget the time,
Joyful moments feel like a rhyme.
Bouncing balls and squeaky shoes,
Counting giggles, we can't lose.

As the sun dips low and shy,
We share our secrets with the sky.
Every chuckle, a tree will hear,
Whispered tales we hold so dear.

Enchanted Merriment

Sprinkled laughter fills the air,
Wandering feet without a care.
Giggling flowers sway in tune,
As whispers dance beneath the moon.

Charming critters play their part,
Painting smiles upon the heart.
With playful prances all around,
Pure delight in every sound.

Bouncing balls and silly games,
Clapping hands and funny names.
Through enchanted woods we run,
Chasing shadows, having fun.

Every twist has us in stitches,
Tickling toes with playful glitches.
In this realm of joy, we roam,
Together, we create our home.

Bubbles of Joy Beneath the Boughs

Bubbles floating through the air,
Every pop, a joyful flare.
Chasing dreams like butterflies,
Sprinkling fun under the skies.

Dancing leaves in happy pairs,
Whirling giggles, light as air.
Round and round, we spin with glee,
In this world, we are so free.

With each splash of giggling light,
The warm sun smiles, oh what a sight!
Ticklish grass beneath our feet,
Every moment, pure and sweet.

As bubbles burst, we dance in sync,
Together, we share a wink.
Joy abounds in every song,
In this place where we belong.

Frisky Flutters of Happiness

Silly antics in sunlight glow,
Frisky flutters, to and fro.
Bouncing bunnies leap around,
Every corner bounds with sound.

Chirping birds sing playful tunes,
Drawing smiles like bright balloons.
In this garden, laughter blooms,
Filling every space with zooms.

Running wild, we chase the breeze,
In this realm, we feel at ease.
With every skip and every hop,
Happiness will never stop.

As shadows stretch with golden rays,
We stand together, lost in play.
Underneath this vibrant sky,
Frisky moments never die.

Glee on the Green

Bouncing balls and laughter fly,
As butterflies flit and zoom by.
A squirrel dances with a glee,
Chasing shadows, wild and free.

Tickles from the soft spring breeze,
Whispers through the leafy trees.
Children chase their dreams in rings,
While hidden gnomes pull silly strings.

A picnic spread with treats galore,
Sandwiches and juice to pour.
With crumbs that spark a tiny race,
Monkeys join the fun, embrace.

Under skies of bright blue cheer,
We laugh until the day draws near.
The sun sets low, as we know best,
In joy, we find our happy rest.

Chuckles Beneath the Branches

Whispers of the breeze conspire,
As laughter lifts, our spirits higher.
A bear with sunglasses makes a scene,
Dancing wildly, oh what a routine!

The parrot mimics silly sounds,
Echoing joy that knows no bounds.
Friends in stone, they grin and wink,
Somewhere nearby, dogs slyly pink.

Pinecones tumble, rolling fast,
Chasing giggles that seem to last.
With every bounce and tumble near,
Nature sways to our delight, dear.

Beneath the branches, spirits glide,
Every moment, a joyful ride.
In this woodland, laughter blooms,
Among the trees, we find our tunes.

Amusement in the Arboretum

Jesters dance upon the grass,
As buds and blooms begin to pass.
Frogs in hats, oh what a sight,
Croaking jokes beneath the light.

Colors splash in playful hues,
Tickling toes and searching clues.
A rooftree race to chase the sun,
With every step, the giggles run.

A bee with stripes tries hard to sing,
While daisies join in on the zing.
Laughter spills, the warmth is near,
In this place, we shed all fear.

With every shade that branches cast,
We know that joy is built to last.
In laughter's arms, we all belong,
From dusk till dawn, it's one sweet song.

Playful Shadows at Dusk

As day fades softly, nights awake,
Whispers rise from every lake.
With shadows dancing, shadows grinning,
The fun begins, the night's just spinning.

A rabbit hops in striped pajamas,
While owls hold court with gleeful dramas.
Fireflies flicker, join the play,
Lighting smiles that drift away.

Behind the trees, jesters blend,
Silly shouts that twist and bend.
The moonlight laughs, a silver spark,
As echoes swirl through the dark.

Under the stars, we sing and prance,
Every moment is a chance.
With hearts so light beneath the glow,
We dance along, in joy, we flow.

Bubbling Bliss in the Brush

In a thicket where shadows play,
The critters dance throughout the day.
Squirrels chatter, making quite a scene,
While rabbits hop in a grassy sheen.

A rustle here, a giggle there,
The wind joins in, light as air.
Leaves tickle noses, a ticklish tease,
As sunlight sparkles between the trees.

Lustre of Laughter Through the Underbrush

Under leaves where whispers flee,
Beneath the boughs, a jolly spree.
Badgers boast of their grand finds,
While hedgehogs grin, with laughter aligned.

A croak of frogs, a chirp of birds,
Funny tales without any words.
Every rustle brings a jest,
Nature's laughter—truly the best.

Wondrous Whimsy of the Woods

Mushrooms caper, colors bright,
Spinning tales in the soft twilight.
Chipmunks tumble, rolling free,
In this realm of pure jubilee.

With every step, surprises greet,
Winging whispers, oh so sweet.
The smallest creatures reign in mirth,
Bringing joy to the forest's girth.

Charming Chuckles in the Change of Season

Leaves turn gold, the air is crisp,
Nature's voice in a cheeky lisp.
Acorns bounce, in playful rows,
Under branches, laughter flows.

Breezes dance with a playful wink,
As creatures plot and nudge and think.
The world's alive, with smiles free,
In every nook, pure glee we see.

www.ingramcontent.com/pod-product-compliance
Lightning Source LLC
Chambersburg PA
CBHW051642160426
43209CB00004B/764